W⊙rk Readiness™

great resume, application, and interview skills

ann byers

ROSEN
PUBLISHING®
New York

Published in 2008 by The Rosen Publishing Group, Inc.
29 East 21st Street, New York, NY 10010

First Edition

Library of Congress Cataloging-in-Publication Data

Byers, Ann.
Great resume, application, and interview skills / Ann Byers.
   p. cm.—(Work readiness)
Includes bibliographical references and index.
ISBN-13: 978-1-4042-1425-5 (library binding)
1. Job hunting—United States. 2. Resumes (Employment)—United States. 3. Applications for positions. 4. Employment interviewing—United States. I. Title.
HF5382.75.U6B94 2008
650.14—dc22

                          2007027293

Manufactured in the United States of America

contents

introduction 4

chapter one Finding a Great Job 6

chapter two Getting Organized 15

chapter three Writing Your Resume 25

chapter four Applications 36

chapter five A Great Interview 45

glossary 56

for more information 58

for further reading 61

bibliography 62

index 63

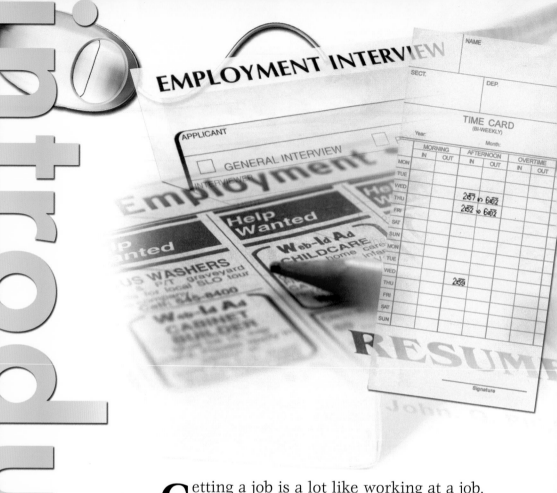

Getting a job is a lot like working at a job. It takes time and effort. It takes skills. And it eventually pays off.

Job-hunting is a two-part process. First you have to find a job that you think you would like. Then you have to actually get that job. The first part, finding the job, takes time and effort. The second part, getting the job, requires skills.

Think about a treasure hunter. To find the treasure he wants, he searches old maps. He reads about where people might have lost or buried their gold or jewels. He studies pictures of the area and listens to old stories. He may join a treasure-hunting club. Only when he knows what he wants and has a pretty good idea where it might be does he go hunting. A lot of time and thought go into the treasure-finding process.

But if he doesn't have the skills, and a few tools, for digging up the treasure, he is not likely to come home with anything of value. In much the same way, without job-hunting skills and tools, you are not likely to get a great job. The tools for the second part of the job-hunting process, actually getting the prize, are resumes, applications, and interviews.

Chapter One

FINDING A GREAT JOB

What do you look for when you want a job? Money? Yes, a job is about making money. But it is also about making a future. It can be part of a career. A job is what you do to make money; a career is what you do to make a life. A career is usually a series of jobs, each a little bigger than the last one. With a little thought and planning, a job hunt can be the beginning of a career.

When you are working full-time, you will spend a third of your day on the job—half the time you are awake. Whether in a job or a career, you probably want to spend that time doing something you enjoy, something you feel good about. So, take some time to figure out what kinds of things you would be happy to do for eight hours a day. Think about what you like to do (your interests), what you are good at (your talents and abilities), and what is important to you (your values).

Your Interests

In considering what you like to do, start with broad categories:

A young employee gets on-the-job training from an experienced baker.

- Do you like to work with people or things?
- Do you want to work with your hands or your mind?
- Would you rather work with others or by yourself?
- Do you like to have a routine or to have things change a lot?
- Do you enjoy doing detail work or not worrying about the little things?
- Do you love to be outside or would you like to work indoors?
- Are you best with lots of activity around you or when things are quiet?

If you really love working with people, you probably will enjoy being a receptionist in a busy office, a server in a restaurant, or working in any number of other positions in which you can meet the public. If you get excited about objects, you might prefer a job as a mechanic, as a computer technician, in a warehouse, or in some place with equipment and machinery. Figuring out what you like to do will help you decide what kind of a job to look for.

What areas of life seem interesting to you? Do you like technology, foods, sports, or recreation? Do health, fitness, and the medical field appeal to you? Does business sound exciting? What about human services, like counseling or social work? Or public services, like police or firefighting? Could you spend all day teaching, building, designing, or making things? Do you like math? Animals? Plants? Technology? You may be able to do a number of different things, but some of these things may rev you up while others seem to drain your energy. You will be happiest when you are in a field that you find exciting.

Many different kinds of jobs are available for people who like working with cars. This young man is checking a car's brakes.

Your Talents and Abilities

You will be happiest doing work you are good at. Everyone has natural talents, things they do well and fairly easily. Some people pick up languages quickly, and some are good at organizing. Some people have an artistic knack, and others are mechanical. Some are born leaders, gifted athletes, or natural actors.

Think about the things you do well. Do you solve puzzles or problems? Can you fix things that are broken? Do your friends ask you to style their hair or do their nails? Do you invent things? Do you like to argue and often win when you do? Are you the one who gets everyone together for a party or project? Are you good at taking care of people? Can you explain complicated things in simple terms? Do you have an eye for fashion? Do you keep careful records? Are you a great driver? You probably have many talents that you have not thought of yet.

Besides your natural talents, you have abilities you have gained through practice. Everyone does not have musical talent, but most people can learn to play the piano. If you are interested in something, you can develop an ability to do it well. Your talents and abilities are important not just in finding a job, but also in getting a job. These are the assets you have to offer an employer.

Your Values

There is more to a job than work and money. Different jobs have different working conditions and different levels of responsibility, freedom, and challenge. In looking at what you might want to do, pay attention to the activities and attitudes that are important to you. If you give up something you value very much to get a particular job, you will not be happy in that job. Some work-related values are the following:

- Helping or influencing others
- Being independent
- Doing something meaningful
- Expressing yourself

Which Job Search Method Works Best?

Job Search Method	Success rate (percent of job seekers who get jobs with this method)	Effectiveness (number of people using this method divided by number of people who find jobs with the method)
Hear about opening from another person	35	33%
Contact employer directly	30	47%
Answer want ads	14	7–12%
Use an employment agency	11	5–28%
Other	10	

From Michael Farr, The Very Quick Job Search: Get a Better Job in Half the Time (Indianapolis, IN: JIST Works, 2004); and Laura Smith-Proulx, Effective Job Search Techniques: Expanding Your Reach Beyond the Internet. Jobing.com (May 23, 2007).

- Power
- Adventure
- Recognition or prestige
- Creativity
- Security
- Not having pressure
- Physical challenge

Any place that has a bulletin board might have a notice of a job opening. Look at bulletin boards in schools, community centers, and public offices.

Which of these values are important to you? Are there others not listed here? Pick your top three and make sure any job you apply for is a good match.

Where to Look

Once you have decided what you want, how do you find it? You can start at your school. Many high schools and colleges have placement offices, career centers, or job counseling offices. These offices often have lists of available jobs and employers who are willing to hire for

"Help Wanted" ads in newspapers often list the qualifications, pay, and work hours of jobs that are available. They tell how and where to apply.

entry-level positions—jobs that require little skill. Placement offices also have tools that can help you identify your interests, abilities, and values. They sometimes offer help in the entire job-hunting process.

You can find some job openings advertised in the "Help Wanted" section of newspapers, in some magazines, and on the Internet. But because these listings are easy to find, lots of people often apply for these jobs. They are harder to get because so many people are applying.

According to the U.S. Bureau of Labor Statistics, at least 80 percent of all jobs are not advertised. About a third of all people with jobs hear about them from someone else. Another third find the employer they want to work for and ask about openings. Laura Smith-Proulx, who has helped many people get high-paying jobs in big companies, says asking about positions even when none are advertised is the best way to find a great job.

If you have a career goal, look for work in that area. You may need more education to reach your goal, but you might find a beginning job in the field. For example, if you want to be an electrician, you could start by working in a hardware store. You might be able to help install some of the appliances that the store sells. If you are planning to become a graphic artist, you can work in a copy shop or printing business. Being a clerk in a floral shop could be the first step to a job as a flower arranger. These entry-level jobs also give you a taste of what a higher-level job in the same field might be like. They help you find out how well you like the career you are considering. They also give you experience and contacts that make it easier to apply for your next position.

After finding the job you want, the next step is getting it!

chapter two

GETTING ORGANIZED

To get the job you want, you need to think like the person who will hire you. What do employers want in the people who work for them? What would you want if someone were working for you? The three top things most employers look for are good attitude, dependability, and skills. Do you have those qualities? How can you show an employer that you are the one who should get the job? You must prove that you are what that employer wants. Take some time to organize all the information you can use to sell yourself.

Your Experience

The most important information you need is what you have done. Think of the jobs you have had and any volunteer work you have participated in. Now, try to recall not the duties you performed, but what you achieved. Not what you did, but what you accomplished. For example, "custodial work" is what someone did; "cleaned and maintained ten offices per week" is what that person accomplished.

Everything you do can be experience. Being in 4-H Club has given this girl experience in caring for animals and accepting responsibility.

The reason your accomplishments are so important is that they predict what you can do. If you built your own bicycle, for example, you can probably repair bicycles in a bike shop. So when you think about your experience, think about what you achieved. If you were a clerk in a clothing store, you did more than just sell clothes. You created a pleasant atmosphere by greeting people, assisted shoppers in finding merchandise, consulted customers about fashion, made suggestions that increased sales, and solved customers' problems. You didn't just do something; you accomplished many things!

If you are looking for your first job, you do not have work history. But you do have experience. Are you involved in sports, clubs, or other activities in school? Do you have hobbies? What school projects did you complete or help with—building a model, making a video report, raising funds? Have you participated in community out-reaches such as painting fences or homes, distributing food to needy families, or cleaning up neighborhoods? What responsibilities do you have at home? Write down everything you can think of that you have accomplished.

Your Skills

Now, you can more clearly figure out what skills you have. Look at your accomplishments. What skills did you use to achieve them? For example, if you worked as a fry cook, you might describe the experience in terms of these achievements:

- Prepared meals for an average of eighty customers per day

This young woman has an entry-level job preparing food orders. This job will give her skills that she can put on her resume for when she applies for her next position.

- Kept track of and prepared multiple orders at a time
- Maintained high-quality food service in fast-paced environment
- Coordinated with other team members to deliver fast, accurate customer service

Do you see how these accomplishments show that you have specific skills? "Prepared meals" shows you have cooking skills. "Kept track of multiple orders" demonstrates the skill of managing several responsibilities simultaneously. "Maintained service in fast-paced environment" illustrates the ability to work under pressure. "Coordinated with team" indicates that you are skilled as a team player.

See? You probably have more skills than you thought!

Education

Your education also suggests what you can do. Maybe you have not accomplished a particular task, but you know how to do it because you have been trained. Think about more than the schools you have attended. Have you had any special training related to the job you are seeking? Did you take any classes that gave you work-related skills, like computer training, auto mechanics, woodworking, or photography? Did you attend any workshops while you were involved in extracurricular activities such as peer counseling, student government, or school newspaper? Write all of this down with the dates of your schooling. This information will become part of your resume.

Letters of Recommendation

All the information in your resume comes from you. It paints a picture of you. Employers usually want to know how other people see you, too. So, they ask for references. You can be one step ahead by having letters of recommendation ready. Do you know people who would be glad to recommend you for a job? They could be teachers, coaches, or people you have worked or volunteered with. Ask them to write letters for you that describe your good qualities. They should write these

Sample Resume

JOHN DOE
111 Main Street
Cleveland, OH
(555) 555-5555
jdoe@ispservices.com

Objective: Auto Parts Counter Person

Summary of Qualifications
• Broad knowledge of auto repair and parts
• Excellent customer relations skills
• Ability to work under pressure
• Willingness to work hard

Relevant Experience
2006–present: Bob's Burgers, Cleveland
• Wait on customers
• Cook and prepare food orders in fast-paced environment
• Advanced from cook to assistant manager in 18 months

2003–present: Repair cars
• Perform minor repairs and tune-ups
• Rebuilt engine of Ford Mustang

Education
Roosevelt High School, Cleveland, OH
Classes in auto mechanics

Computer skills are needed for many different types of jobs. Computer classes will look good on almost any resume.

letters on business letterhead so that they will look professional.

Make copies of all your letters of recommendation because you don't want to lose the originals. If they are on letterhead with color, you might want to spend the extra money to have color copies made.

Cover Letters

Any time you give your resume or letters of recommendation to a prospective employer, you will need a cover

Cover Letter Template

Your street address
Your city, state, and ZIP code
Date you are writing

Name and title of person you are writing to
Company name
Street address of company
City, state, and ZIP of company

Dear Personnel Manager:

I am enclosing my resume in response to your advertisement in
_____ on (date) for the position of _____.

As my resume shows, I have had experience etc., etc., etc.

I would like the opportunity of talking with you about this position at your earliest convenience. I can be reached at (your phone number). I will call you at the beginning of next week if I have not heard from you before then.

Sincerely,

Your handwritten signature

Your name

letter. A cover letter is a letter that goes on top of, or covers, a more important document. It is an introduction. Sending a resume without a cover letter is like bursting into a room of strangers and starting to talk without even saying who you are. It is very brief, no more than three short paragraphs. It tells the person receiving your document why you are sending it, who you are, and exactly what you want.

A cover letter is a business letter, so it has both your address and the address of the company to which you are sending it. Never send a letter to "To whom it may concern" or "Dear sir or madam." Try to find the name of the person doing the hiring. You can call the company and ask for the name. Make sure you have the correct spelling. Even a common name like Smith can be spelled more than one way. If you cannot find the name, address your letter to the Personnel Manager or Hiring Director.

Look at the cover letter template on page 22. The letter is very simple. The first paragraph says that you are writing to apply for a particular position. It mentions how you heard about the opening. The second paragraph highlights your qualifications for the job. These qualifications will be detailed in your resume. The last paragraph asks for an interview. Getting an interview is what every piece of paper is about.

After you write a cover letter, print it out and read it over carefully. Compare it with the template. Is the punctuation correct? Is the spacing the same? Are all the words spelled correctly? Don't rely on the spell-check feature of your computer. Both "skill" and "spill" are words, but if you want people to know you are experienced in several types of painting, you don't want them to read that you have "a variety of paint spills."

When you have organized the information that will go into the picture you will paint of yourself for a prospective employer, you are ready to write a great resume.

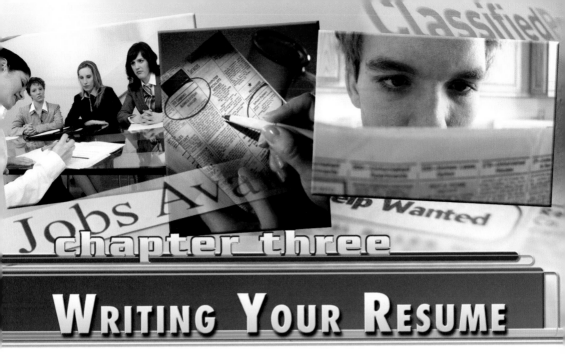

chapter three

WRITING YOUR RESUME

For many jobs, your resume is your first chance to sell yourself. The purpose of your resume is to make an employer interested enough to interview you. A resume is a screening tool. Like a screen on a window, its purpose is to keep things out. A resume screens out people the employer does not want to interview. A good resume by itself will not get you a job, but a bad resume can keep you from getting one.

In writing your resume, you must think like the person who will be reading it. Employers may have a lot of resumes to read, and they read them very quickly. They are not reading them to get to know anyone; they are reading to see whom they can eliminate. Your resume has to show them, within about a minute, that you are able to do the job.

Contact Information

Your resume begins with your name and the information needed to contact you: address, telephone number, and

This man is holding resumes that he received from one day at a job fair. If your resume were in this stack, would it stand out?

e-mail address. If your e-mail address sounds "cute" or suggestive, you may not want to include it. What might employers think if they try to reach you at something like "babyface@hotmail.com"? Look at everything on your resume the way a prospective employer would.

Objective

The first line the employer will read should be your employment objective. This is a short description of the job you are seeking. It can be simply the name of the position for which you are applying such as "Appliance Installer" or "Data Entry Clerk." Or it can be a description of the type of job: "Customer Service Position."

Your job objective should be specific. If you are applying for different jobs at different companies, prepare a separate resume for each one. The rest of your resume will demonstrate that you have the abilities to perform the specific job that you give as your objective.

Summary of Qualifications

The main information an employer is looking for is your ability to do the job—your qualifications. This section is very important. It shows that you have thought seriously about the job and believe you have what it takes to do it. It tells employers why they should hire you.

Your skills will show up in your "Experience" section, but you have to make sure the person reading your resume does not miss them. So, even though you mention them later, you still need to state your qualifications very clearly and briefly right at the start. Employers scanning resumes quickly may not even get to the "Experience" section. Remember, they are reading resumes to screen people out. If you list your qualifica- tions well at the beginning, the employer will be more likely to pay attention to your experience to see if you have shown that you do, indeed, have those abilities.

Experience/Relevant Skills

There are two ways to describe your experience: as employment history or as relevant skills. If you are doing an employment history, list the places you have worked, starting with your current or most recent job, and go backward. Give the dates you worked, the name of the company, and the job title.

Don't stop there. Job titles do not tell what you accomplished. And your accomplishments, not your responsibilities, are what matter to an employer. So, under each job, describe two or more achievements. Begin each with an action word such as "developed," "presented," "organized," or "planned." Verbs are more powerful than nouns, and you want your accomplishments to sound strong.

What if you have little or no work history? Then you call this section "Relevant Skills" or "Relevant Experience." List the skills that the job calls for and, under each skill, describe your accomplishments in that area. Look at the sample resume on page 20. Every qualification listed is backed up with an achievement in the "Relevant Experience" section.

When employers look at your work history, they often are looking for more than the jobs you have held. They may want to know how long you stayed at each one. Remember that one of the things employers look for is dependability. If they see that you moved from job to job, they will question how dependable you are going to be for them. If you had several jobs for brief periods, you can make this a little less obvious by dividing the "Experience" section into two parts: "Relevant Skills" and "Employment History." Under "Employment History," simply list your jobs. Concentrate on making the "Relevant Skills" part sharp.

What is wrong with this resume? What does the reader see first? You want the first words noticed to be your name. Do not write the word "resume" on your resume.

Formatting

Some word-processing programs have templates you can use to format your resume. However, these templates may not have the sections you need. And working with templates can be tricky. Creating your own professional-looking resume is actually very simple.

Set the page with one-inch margins all around. If your resume ends up being too short, you can increase the margins later. Choose a standard font such as Times

New Roman, Courier, or Ariel. Nothing fancy. Do not use more than one type of font. Point 12 is an easy-to-read size. If you go much larger, it looks as if you do not have much to say and are trying to fill empty space.

Begin with your name and contact information. You can center this or arrange it flush left (every line even with the left margin). Make your name stand out by putting it in boldface. You might also use a slightly larger font or type your name in all capital letters. Below your name, on separate lines, type your address (takes two lines), phone number, and e-mail address.

Next you will place the "Objective," "Summary of Qualifications," "Experience" (or "Relevant Skills"), and "Education" sections. To make each section easy for the reader to find, put the titles in boldface and leave spaces between sections. In a short document, titles that are flush left are generally easier to spot than titles that are centered.

Within each section, use short phrases instead of complete sentences. Employers want to get to the point quickly, so leave out any unnecessary words. Beginning each phrase with a bullet gives a sharp look and organizes the items nicely. Because bulleted items are not sentences, do not put a period after them.

Polishing

Now that you have a great resume, let's be sure it looks great. Print a copy. What is your first thought when you see it? Is it neat and attractive? Do you notice the headings right away? Does your name stand out? Do the words seem balanced on the page, rather than bunched

Prospective employers often begin with your resume when they interview you. They may ask you to give details about what you wrote on your resume.

up in spots? Does it look like something you would want to read?

If it seems too plain, you can dress it up a little with a plain horizontal line all the way across the page (inside the margins) under your contact information. Use just a simple line, and nothing more than a line. You want it to look professional, not fancy.

When you are pleased with the general appearance, read it over critically. Look for any capitalization, punctuation, and spelling mistakes. See if any spaces are uneven. When you are satisfied, ask other people to read

Sample Electronic Resume

JOHN DOE
111 Main Street
Cleveland, OH
(555) 555-5555
jdoe@ispservices.com

SKILLS SUMMARY
Knowledgeable in automotive repair, auto parts, mechanics; front-counter experience; customer relations skills; hard worker; courteous under pressure

EXPERIENCE
2006–present: Bob's Burgers, Cleveland
- Customer service provider
- Cook
- Order fulfillment—took and filled orders
- Assistant manager—advanced to position in 18 months

2003–present: Automotive Maintenance and Repair
- Repairs and tune-ups
- Engine rebuilding—rebuilt Ford Mustang engine

EDUCATION
Roosevelt High School, Cleveland, OH
- Auto mechanics

it and tell you honestly what they think. If you make any changes, read the entire resume over again.

Print your final copies on good paper—something just a little stiffer than regular copier paper. White, ivory, and off-white colors are professional looking and are thus good for resumes. You don't need to put them in report covers or notebooks. Keep them—unfolded—in a hard-sided folder or notepad, ready to take out and hand to a prospective employer.

Electronic Resumes

In today's age of technology, you may not be able to hand your resume to an employer. Instead of a paper resume, a company may ask for a scannable, or electronic, resume.

A scannable resume is one that can be converted to electronic form. A computer uses a scanner to "read" your resume and change it from print to computer language. Then, the employers do not have to read every resume they receive. They can scan all of them at once, telling their computers to look for certain words, called keywords. The computers can arrange in order all the resumes that have those particular words, with the best on top. The best are usually the ones with the most keywords.

So, the secret to a great scannable resume is having the right keywords. What words do employers look for? They look for skill words, words that suggest you can do the job. If you are asked for a scannable resume, you need to pack it with skill words. In fact, the "Summary of Qualifications" section needs to be changed to "Summary

A computer makes it easy to change your resume and cover letters when you are applying to different companies or for different jobs.

of Skills" or "Keyword Summary." You do not need to state an objective because the scanner is looking for skills and it simply will skip over the word "objective."

This means that some of the verbs you used in your paper resume have to be changed to nouns. Therefore, "planned events" becomes "event planner" and "trained packers" becomes "packing house trainer." How do you know which keywords a hirer is scanning for? Check the job advertisements for words that are used often by employers in the type of job for which you are applying.

The formatting has to be changed as well. Scanners cannot read bullets, italics, boldface, lines, centering, or anything else that is not plain text. So, put the entire resume flush left. Change everything that was set in bold or italics to simple print. Keep the spaces between your sections, and put the section titles in all capital letters. In place of bullets, type a hyphen (-); scanners can read a hyphen because it is on the computer keyboard.

Now, armed with a paper and a scannable resume, you are ready to fill out the employment application.

chapter four

APPLICATIONS

Some jobs do not require resumes, but nearly every job requires an application. Like a resume, an application is a screening tool that separates the "maybes" from the "definitely nots." Like a resume, it may very well be the first impression that a prospective employer has of you. Even before reading what you have written on the application, an employer will form ideas about you by simply looking at the application you have filled out.

Think like an employer. What does a piece of paper tell you about the person who handed it to you? A smudged or messy page suggests that the person does not have a respectful attitude. Sloppy handwriting says the person is not careful. A lot of erasures or crossed-out words imply that the person does not think clearly. Empty spaces say the person does not have much to offer. Would you hire a person who gave you a messy application? Not likely. The way your application looks does not tell your many positive qualities, but it can practically shout some negative traits if they are there. Taking a little time, in preparing for the application as well as in filling it out, is well worth the effort.

Every company has its own application form, but some items are fairly standard. Learn what these items are and write down your responses to them. Take the paper with your responses—we'll call it a "help sheet"—when you are job hunting. That way, you will be ready to fill out an application easily and quickly.

You might have other papers to carry also: copies of your resume, letters of recommendation, and examples of the work you have done. If you put them all in a hard-sided folder or notepad, you will keep them neat and clean. Besides, when you come into an office or business carrying a nice notebook, you look much more professional than if you pull a folded piece of paper out of your pocket. How you look is just as important as how your application looks!

The Application Form

Most applications ask for five types of information: (1) personal information about you, (2) information about the position and your fitness for the job, (3) your education, (4) your experience, and (5) who can recommend you for the job.

- **Personal information.** In addition to your name, you will need your Social Security number. You may have to give your driver's license number and proof of citizenship. It is a good idea to have these identification cards with you in case the person receiving your application wants to attach copies. Along with your address, you might be asked how long you have lived at that location. If less than a

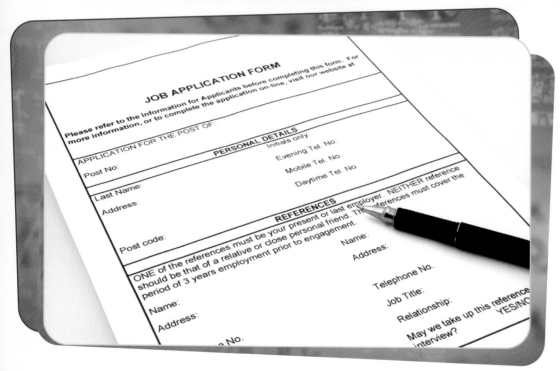

Some applications have very little space for you to write your answers. Before you start to write, think of exactly what you want to say.

year, you might have to give the same information for the place you lived before your current address. Write all of this down on your help sheet.

- **Position applied for.** Companies often use one application for many different jobs, so the application usually asks what position you are applying for. Give the exact name of the job if you know it. If you heard about an opening through a job listing or advertisement, bring that with you so that you can write the name with no mistakes. Sometimes an application asks how you heard of the opening, so have that information with you, too. Be as exact as you can. If you saw an ad in a newspaper, write the name of the paper.

Not every job is a permanent, full-time position. Some are seasonal (for a short, specific period of time) and some are temporary (until a task is finished). Others are part-time. Think about whether you are willing to accept seasonal, temporary, or part-time work. That question may be on the application. Another question that may be asked, especially for a company that has different shifts, is what days and hours you are available.

You may see a line for "expected salary" or "lowest rate of pay you will accept." Like all the other items, this is a screening question. You don't want to be screened out by giving a figure that is too high, but you don't want a job that pays too low. If you can, research the company or the type of job before you apply and get an idea of what people are getting paid in that position. If you cannot find out anything, you can write "open" or "negotiable." This means you are willing to talk about pay. It is not a specific answer, so it does not screen you out.

Applications often ask if you have any physical conditions that limit you in doing certain kinds of work. If you say "yes," you are not automatically screened out. It is illegal to deny you a job because of physical disabilities. But you do have to tell about any limitations you have and describe how they affect your ability to work. If you are limited in one area, you can work in another.

Carry an ink pen and your help sheet when you are job hunting so you are ready to fill out the application form with confidence.

- **Education.** Applications often ask for names of the schools you attended (high school and above), the dates you attended each, and whether you graduated. Sometimes they want your grade point average (GPA) and the number of credits you earned. These are a lot of numbers to remember, so having them on your help sheet will make filling out the application much easier. If you received a General Educational Development (GED) certificate instead of a diploma, you can give that information. Be prepared to list any certifications you have and the dates they were issued or the dates they expire.

- **Experience.** Applications generally have space for you to list all of the jobs you have had for the past five years or longer. In addition to the names and addresses of companies, the titles of the positions, and the dates worked, make sure you have the names and phone numbers of your supervisors on those jobs. Also be ready to write down the amount of money you were paid. Applications often ask about the pay when you started the job and the pay when you left, as you may have gotten raises. If the item says "earnings per _____," you decide whether to put how much you earned per year, per month, per week, or per hour. You might want to have the figure for each on your help sheet.

A common question you may not expect is, "About how many days have you been absent from your job because of sickness?" You may be asked to explain.

Employers want to know why you left or are considering leaving another job. Try to express your reasons for leaving in a positive way. Remember, employers want people with good attitudes. You might say (if these are the real reasons) "to seek a more challenging opportunity," "to find full-time work," or "to explore a different field."

Employers who decide to consider you usually will call your previous supervisors. They want to know how dependable and skilled you are. They also are trying to find out how well you get along with other people. They understand that you may not want your current employer to know that you are looking for another job. So, where the application asks "May we contact your present employer?" it is perfectly all right for you to write "Not yet."

- **References.** In addition to previous supervisors, what other people will recommend you to an employer? You need to think of four or five because you surely will be asked for the names of at least three. They cannot be family members. They can be teachers, neighbors, coaches, or friends. They can be people you worked with, but not the supervisors you list in the "Experience" section. Make sure to ask these people if you can use them as references. If they say "yes" and seem genuinely happy to recommend you, write their addresses and phone numbers on your help sheet.

- **Other questions.** Applications often have spaces where you can list special skills, hobbies, or interests. Be as specific as you can, especially if you have skills that are relevant to the job. Instead of "computer skills," for example, name the computer programs you can operate.

Filling Out the Form

Whenever you are job-hunting, be ready to fill out an application on the spot. In addition to your help sheet and resumes, carry a black ink pen with you. You might want to have an ink eraser or Wite-Out (correction fluid) just in case you make a mistake.

This young man is having trouble with a question on a job application. Writing answers down ahead of time makes filling out the application easier.

The biggest mistake people make on the application is not following directions. Read the instructions carefully. If they say to use black ink, do not use blue. If they say to print, then print. If they say, "Do not leave any space blank," you had better fill in everything. Remember, it is a screening tool, and a poorly filled out application will screen you out.

Even if the directions do not say so, try not to leave any blanks. If a question does not seem to apply to you, simply write "not applicable" or "N.A."

When you are finished filling out the form, read it over again to make sure it is clear and accurate. If any question confuses you, write the question and your answer on your help sheet. Any unusual item is likely to come up in an interview. And the interview is the next step!

chapter five

A GREAT INTERVIEW

The interview is what the other parts of the job-getting process are about. Resumes, applications, and references all are done to get you to the interview. They are screens, used to weed people out. The purpose of the interview is to get someone in.

For a great interview, like a great resume, you have to think like the employer. What are employers looking for when they meet you? Your resume and application say that maybe you can do the job. In the interview, you have to convince them that you really can. You also have to convince them that you are dependable and that you will fit in their company.

Look Great

Employers are sizing you up from the moment you walk in the room. When they see you, you want them to think, "Here is someone I would like to see at my business." Of course, you will be neat and clean. Pay attention to the small details of your grooming, like your fingernails.

The young woman interviewing for a job appears comfortable and confident. She is listening intently and looking her interviewer in the eye.

What should you wear? You might take a trip to the office or plant where you hope to be working, sit outside, and watch how people who work there dress. Then dress just a little more nicely. Don't make your scouting trip on a Friday, when many companies have "casual" or "dress-down" day. Think of an interview as a special occasion and dress up. That means no tank tops, sandals, tennis shoes, low-cut tops, or jeans. Guys probably want to wear a suit or slacks, a button-down shirt, a tie, and a jacket or sports coat. Women should wear a business suit or dress or a simple skirt with a nice blouse.

Even if the job you are applying for does not require dressy clothes, a business suit is nearly always the right outfit for an interview.

Make sure you are not wearing anything distracting. You want the interviewer to focus on your abilities and attitude, not on how you look. That means no flashy jewelry, bright fingernail polish, or wild hairstyles. Better leave off the perfume or cologne, or at least go lightly—your interviewer could be allergic to certain odors. Speaking of odors, you might want to pop a breath mint in your mouth while you are waiting for the interviewer to call you in.

Act Great

You will be waiting because you will have arrived early. "On time" for an interview means at least ten minutes before it is scheduled to start.

Being on time and all the other things you do at the beginning of an interview tell a lot about you. You will feel nervous, but remind yourself that you can do this job. You are happy to finally have the chance to convince your prospective employer that you can do it. You look great, you are prepared, and you are eager to show the interviewer who you are and what you can do. Thinking like this will help you feel confident, and interviewers like confident people.

Three actions say you are confident: smiling, making eye contact, and giving a firm handshake. When you smile, you look like you are happy to be at the interview. When you look the interviewer in the eye, you show that you are not afraid of him or her. And a solid handshake makes you appear strong. These three simple actions go a long way toward making a great first impression.

10 Great Questions to Ask

1. Do I know what kind of job I would like and would be good at?

2. Am I convinced that I can do the job? (If not, how can I convince someone else?)

3. Can someone look at my resume and tell in one minute what I have done and what I can do?

4. Do the qualifications I list on my resume match the skills needed for the job?

5. Do the accomplishments I list on my resume match the qualifications I listed?

6. Does my resume have words commonly used in the field for which I am applying?

7. Do I have a scannable resume as well as a paper one?

8. Do I have the names, addresses, and phone numbers—and permission—of at least three people who will give me good recommendations?

9. What do I know about the company I am applying to?

10. Am I dressed nicely for an interview?

Throughout the interview, take your cues from the interviewer. Stand until the interviewer sits or invites you to sit.

A seemingly silly but very real concern is what to do with your hands. Hand movements can betray nervousness and they can be distracting. One way to take care of this issue is to bring something with you that you can hold. Remember the folder or notepad you use for keeping copies of your resumes? Bring that and add paper and pen for taking notes.

Prepare Well

You should be taking notes before you even get to the interview. You need to know as much about the company as you can. What are its mission and vision? What products does it make? What services does it offer? Who are its customers? How well is it doing? Who does it compete with? You can learn these things by looking at the company's Web site, reading the company's literature, and reading articles in newspapers and magazines. If you can, talk with someone who works for the company. The more you know about the business, the better you can answer and ask questions.

To make sure you will be on time, plan how you will get there. If you are going by car, drive the route ahead of time so you know how long it takes. Plan alternate routes in case your way is blocked. If you will be taking a bus or another form of public transportation, make a practice trip a day or two before. Whether you are going by car or public transportation, try to do your dry run at the same time of day you will be traveling for

This young woman appears prepared for her interview. She is dressed in a business suit and has extra copies of her resume.

your interview. Traffic can be different at different times of the day. You don't want any surprises. Just in case something you can't imagine happens and you are late, you should have with you the name and phone number of someone at the company.

The night before your interview, get everything ready. Iron your clothes, shine your shoes, and organize your folder or notepad. You will want to have extra resumes and copies of anything that shows your skills: letters of recommendation, awards, and materials you have produced. Make copies you can leave with the interviewer; do not give anyone your originals.

Common Interview Questions

- Tell me a little about yourself.
- What is one of your greatest strengths?
- What is one of your weaknesses?
- What did you like best about your last job?
- Why did you apply for this job?
- What excites you about the job?
- What about the job will be challenging for you?
- What plans do you have for your future?
- What will your former coworkers say about you?
- Why should I hire you?

Questions to Ask the Interviewer

- Who will I be reporting to?
- What opportunities will I have for advancement?
- Why is this job open?
- How will this company be different five years from now?
- What are the specific responsibilities of the job?

Show What You Can Do

The heart of the interview is, of course, the questions you are asked. The purpose of the questions is to see how well you can do the job. So, as you answer, try to relate your achievements to the skills needed to do the job. For example, if you are asked if you are comfortable working in a fast-paced environment, do not merely say,

Whether you think the interview went well or poorly, leave with the same confident smile, eye contact, and firm handshake you had at the beginning of the interview.

"Yes." Talk about a time when you did work in such an environment.

An interviewer might ask how you enjoyed working at a past job. If that job was a negative experience for you, try to put it in a positive light: "It was difficult, but it taught me to be more assertive." Turn your negatives into learning experiences.

The interviewer will give you a chance to ask questions also. You should ask two or three because if you have no questions, you will appear uninterested in the job. You can ask about the company, showing that

Taking time to develop great resume, application, and interview skills paid off for this young woman, who has achieved her job objective. She is working at a clothing store, beginning a career as a fashion consultant.

you took the time to learn something about it. Or you can ask about job duties. Whatever you do, do not ask about salary! That question can make an interviewer think you do not care about anything else. The time to ask about pay is when you are offered the job.

Follow Up

Before you leave the interview, try to get a business card with the interviewer's name on it. If you can't get a card, write down the person's name and title. Ask the receptionist for that information if you need to, and be sure to get the correct spelling. Nothing makes a worse impression than spelling a person's name incorrectly! You will need this information for a thank-you letter.

As soon as you leave the interview, write a letter to the interviewer. Thank the interviewer for taking time to consider you for the position, and repeat your skills/qualifications for the job. Mail it right away. Then wait.

Give the employer five to ten days after receiving your thank-you letter. If you do not hear from the employer in that time, call to say you are checking on the status of the position opening.

And then you may have to wait some more. Spend your waiting time exploring other job openings.

Do not get discouraged if you do not get an interview right away. Do not be frustrated if you are not offered a job after a great interview. Remember that getting a job is as much work as having a job. Polish your resume, practice your skills, and keep at it. Your hard work will eventually pay off!

glossary

applicant Person applying for a job.

asset An item, ability, or quality that has value. A person's talents, skills, education, and experience can be assets to an employer.

bullet Graphic device used to designate items in a list. A bullet is usually a dot, and it is placed at the beginning of each item.

cover letter A letter that is sent with a resume or other document introducing the document. When job applicants send resumes to a prospective employer, they should send a cover letter with each one.

entry-level Refers to a beginning job in any field, a job that does not require much skill or knowledge.

flush left Even with the left margin of the paper.

horizontal Straight across from side to side, like the horizon (where the sky and the earth or sea seem to meet).

keyword Word or phrase employers look for on electronic resumes. Keywords are usually words that describe a job applicant's skills or experience.

letterhead Stationery that has the name and address of a business printed on it and that is used by businesses for letters.

placement office Department in a school that helps students find jobs. Counselors in placement offices usually have listings of job openings and ideas that help students locate and get jobs.

prospective employer Person who is not your employer now but who may become your employer in the future.

relevant skills Abilities that have to do with the job for which you are applying.

scannable resume Resume that can be converted by a
computer scanner from print to electronic form.

screening process Method that a prospective employer
uses to eliminate applicants from consideration for
employment.

template Preset form that is used to create a document.

Career Lab
10475 Park Meadows Drive, Suite 600
Lone Tree, CO 80124-5437
(303) 790-0505
Web site: http://www.careerlab.com
A career strategy and development company that provides
    samples of all types of cover letters.

Job Futures: Canada's National Career and Education
    Planning Tool
Service Canada
140 Promenade du Portage, Phase IV
Hull, QC K1A 0J9
Canada
(800) 622-6232
Web site: http://www.jobfutures.ca/en/home.shtml
A service of the national government of Canada, offering
    an interest assessment and information about
    occupations, schools, and trade organizations.

National Career Development Association
305 N. Beech Circle
Broken Arrow, OK 74012
(910) 663-7060
Web site: http://ncda.org
This organization provides links to many career resources
    such as interest assessments and information about
    different occupations and salaries.

Professional Association of Resume Writers and Career
    Coaches
1388 Brightwaters Boulevard NE

St. Petersburg, FL 33704

(727) 821-2274 or (800) 822-7279

Web site: http://www.parw.com

This organization and online site enables you to search for resume writers, interview professionals, and career coaches in your geographic area.

University of Waterloo

200 University Avenue West

Waterloo, ON N2L 3G1

Canada

(519) 888-4567

Web site: http://www.cdm.uwaterloo.ca

The university's Web site offers an online career development manual with step-by-step instructions for building a resume.

U.S. Bureau of Labor Statistics (BLS)

U.S. Department of Labor

Postal Square Building

2 Massachusetts Avenue NE

Washington, DC 20212-0001

(202) 691-5200

Web site: http://www.bls.gov/home.htm; for *Occupational Outlook Handbook* Online: http://www.bls.gov/oco/

The BLS is the main fact-finding agency for the U.S. government in the field of labor economics and statistics. It describes various jobs and careers, and offers career-related help for high school students at http://www.bls.gov/k12/index.htm. It also publishes the *Occupational Outlook Handbook*, which gives descriptions of 250 occupations: what each job is like, what training is needed, what it pays, as well as the working conditions and what the future of that job looks like.

Web Sites

Due to the changing nature of Internet links, Rosen Publishing has developed an online list of Web sites related to the subject of this book. The site is updated regularly. Please use this link to access the list:

http://www.rosenlinks.com/wr/rais

for further reading

Bolles, Richard Nelson, Carol Christen, and Jean M.
Blomquiest. *What Color Is Your Parachute for Teens:
Discovering Yourself, Defining Your Future*. Berkeley,
CA: Ten Speed Press, 2006.

Coon, Nora. *Teen Dream Jobs: How to Find the Job You
Really Want Now!* Hillsboro, OR: Beyond Words, 2003.

Culbreath, Alice N., and Saundra K. Neal. *Testing the
Waters: A Teen's Guide to Career Exploration*. Jupiter,
FL: Jrc Consulting, 1999.

Delano, Molly. *Summer Jobs and Opportunities for Teenagers:
A Planning Guide*. Cambridge, MA: Da Capo, 2001.

Farr, Michael J., Marie A. Pavlicko, and Gayle O.
Macdonald. *Young Person's Guide to Getting and
Keeping a Good Job*. 2d ed. Indianapolis, IN: JIST
Works, 2000.

Foster, Chad. *Teenagers Preparing for the Real World*.
Boston, MA: Southwestern Educational, 1998.

Harbeke, Dan. *Get In! How to Market Yourself and
Become Successful at a Young Age*. Lanham, MD:
Scarecrow, 2003.

Pervola, Cindy, and Debby Hobgood. *How to Get a Job if
You're a Teenager*. Ft. Atkinson, WI: Highsmith, 1998.

Schwartz, Stuart, and Craig Conley. *Considering a Job
Offer*. Mankato, MN: Capstone, 1999.

Vernon, Naomi. *A Teen's Guide to Finding a Job*. San
Antonio, TX: New Bee-ginnings, 2000.

Wright, Dixie L. *Know-How Is the Key: Job Smarts for
Students with Learning and Other Disabilities*.
Indianapolis, IN: JIST Works, 1997.

bibliography

Bloch, Deborah. *Get Your First Job and Keep It*. New York, NY: McGraw-Hill, 2002.

Farr, Michael. *Getting the Job You Really Want*. Indianapolis, IN: JIST Works, 2002.

Farr, Michael. *The Very Quick Job Search: Get a Better Job in Half the Time*. Indianapolis, IN: JIST Works, 2004.

McKay, Dawn Rosenberg. *The Everything Get-A-Job Book*. Avon, MA: Adams Media, 2007.

Smith-Proulx, Laura. "Effective Job Search Techniques: Expanding Your Reach Beyond the Internet." May 22, 2007. Retrieved June 1, 2007 (http://phoenix.jobing.com/blog_post.asp?post=4560).

index

A

applications, job, 36–44, 45
    information requested on,
      37–42

C

cover letter, 21–24

D

dependability, 15, 28, 41

E

education
    listing in resume, 30
    listing on application, 40–41
    organizing information, 19
electronic resumes, 32, 33–35
employment history/experience
    listing in resume, 27–28
    listing on application, 41–42
    organizing information
      about, 15–17

I

interests, figuring out your, 6–8
interviews, 45–55
    common questions asked,
      52, 53
    following up after, 54–55
    how to act during, 48–50
    personal appearance, 45–48
    preparing for, 50–51
    questions to ask, 52, 53–54

J

job search, 4–5, 11
    information to gather for,
      15–24
    things to consider, 6–14

L

letters of recommendation,
    19–21, 37, 51

R

references, 19, 42, 45
resumes, 25–35
    contact information in,
      25–26, 30
    electronic, 32, 33–35
    experience/skills in,
      27–28, 30
    formatting of, 29–30, 31, 35
    objective in, 26–27, 30, 34
    polishing, 30–33
    summary of qualifications
      in, 27, 30, 33–34

S

skills
    listing in resume, 27–28, 30
    listing on application, 42
    organizing information
      about, 17–19

V

values, work-related, 10–12

About the Author

As director of a youth program, Ann Byers has examined resumes, conducted interviews, and hired people for a variety of management, entry-level, intern, and volunteer positions. She has coached young people through the entire job search process and has written resumes as well as interview questions. Byers knows what employers look for and how to show them you have it!

Photo Credits

Cover (top left, top right, bottom middle, bottom right) © Shutterstock.com; cover (top middle) © www.istockphoto.com; cover (middle, left to right) © www.istockphoto.com/anne stahl, © www.istockphoto.com/Joan Kimball; cover (bottom left) © www.istockphoto.com/Steve Pepple; pp. 6, 15, 25, 36, 45 (left to right) © Steve Pepple/www.istockphoto.com, © www.istockphoto.com/James Courtney, © www.istockphoto.com/Karen Squires; p. 7 © www.istockphoto.com/Willie B. Thomas; p. 9 © www.istockphoto.com/Christopher Pattberg; p. 12 © Dana White/Photo Edit; © www.istockphoto.com/Michak Rozanski; p. 16 © AP/Wide World Photos; p. 18 © Elena Roorald/Photo Edit; pp. 21, 26 © Getty Images; p. 29 © www.istockphoto.com/Jim Jurica; p. 31 © www.istockphoto.com/Stefan Klein; p. 34 © David Young-Wolff/Photo Edit; p. 38 © www.istockphoto.com; p. 40 © www.istockphoto.com/Rob Friedman; p. 43 © Spencer Grant/Photo Edit; p. 46 © www.istockphoto.com/Amanda Rohde; p. 47 © www.istockphoto.com/Diane Diederich; p. 51 © www.istockphoto.com/Sean Locke; pp. 53, 54 © Shutterstock.com.

Designer: Nelson Sá; **Editor:** Kathy Campbell
Photo Researcher: Marty Levick